The Sermon on the Mount

A Twenty-One-Day Devotional Study

ARMONDO L. JACKSON

THE SERMON ON THE MOUNT
A TWENTY-ONE-DAY DEVOTIONAL STUDY

iUniverse books may be ordered through booksellers or by contacting:

iUniverse
1663 Liberty Drive
Bloomington, IN 47403
www.iuniverse.com
1-800-Authors (1-800-288-4677)

Because of the dynamic nature of the Internet, any web addresses or links contained in this book may have changed since publication and may no longer be valid. The views expressed in this work are solely those of the author and do not necessarily reflect the views of the publisher, and the publisher hereby disclaims any responsibility for them.

Any people depicted in stock imagery provided by Getty Images are models, and such images are being used for illustrative purposes only. Certain stock imagery © Getty Images.

Scripture quotations marked KJV are from the Holy Bible, King James Version (Authorized Version). First published in 1611. Quoted from the KJV Classic Reference Bible, Copyright © 1983 by The Zondervan Corporation.

Scripture quoted by permission. Quotations designated (NET) are from The NET Bible® Copyright © 2005 by Biblical Studies Press, L.L.C. www.bible.org All rights reserved.

The ESV® text has been reproduced in cooperation with and by permission of Good News Publishers. Unauthorized reproduction of this publication is prohibited. All rights reserved.

ISBN: 978-1-6632-0073-0 (sc)
ISBN: 978-1-6632-0072-3 (e)

Library of Congress Control Number: 2020912163

Print information available on the last page.

iUniverse rev. date: 07/14/2020

CONTENTS

INTRODUCTION

"What word or phrase would you use to absolutely capture the essence of Jesus' teaching?" This was the question New Testament scholar Gordon Fee asked a class of forty seminary students during a course on the life and teaching of Jesus. Out of forty students, Fee recalls, only three gave the answer he was looking for. Most students gave answers such as "love" or "forgiveness". The best answer, however, is "the kingdom of God" (or kingdom of heaven in Matthew's gospel). The abiding theme in the teaching of Jesus is the kingdom of heaven (see Matt. 4:17; 5:3, 10, 19; 7:21; 8:11; 10:7; 13:11).

The Sermon on the Mount outlines the character requirements and expectations for those who are citizens of the kingdom of heaven. It is Jesus' most extensive teaching recorded in the gospels. In the gospel of Matthew, it spans three entire chapters (Matthew 5 – 7). The background to the sermon is typological to Moses and the people of Israel in their wilderness wanderings and at Mount Sinai. Moses and the people of Israel spent forty years in the wilderness and were tested as they wandered in the desert. Jesus has just emerged victorious from a forty day fast (1 day for each year) in the desert wilderness and did not fail as he faced similar tests and temptations (4:1 – 11).

Jesus succeeded in every area where the people of Israel failed. The people of Israel complained about food and began missing the food of Egypt (Exodus 16:1 – 3). Jesus refused to eat food illegitimately (Matt 4:3 – 4). The people of Israel tested the Lord (Exodus 17:1 – 3). Jesus refused to put God to the test (Matt 4:7). Finally, the people of Israel bowed down and worshiped an idol (Exodus 32:1 – 6). Jesus refused to bow down to the devil (Matt 4:9 – 10). Moses went up Mount Sinai to receive instruction from God. From the mountain, Moses delivered God's Word to the people of Israel. Likewise, Jesus positioned himself on the side of a mountain and gave this remarkable sermon to his disciples.

Matthew records the sermon as occurring close to the beginning of Jesus' ministry and thus it sets the stage for what follows. It covers a variety of topics and touches on several key themes that will come up again later in the gospel. What follows is a twenty-one day devotional study of the sermon. All referenced Bible verses are my own translation from the NA28 Greek New Testament. I have used footnotes to provide additional information such as grammatical observations and historical notes that can be used for further study. This devotional is designed to provide insight into the sermon that can be used for practical application in our walk with God. I pray that God blesses you through it.

My wife Dione was the first person to read through the entire devotional. I printed out a copy and asked for her candid feedback. She read it through like a true devotional, reading and meditating on one section per day. I noticed that she had written a personal prayer at the end of some of the devotionals. I was given permission to include some of those prayers here in the book version. Each entry includes a reflection.

DAY 1

"Who are You Really?"
(Matthew 5:1 – 3)

And seeing the crowds, he went up the mountain and after he sat down his disciples came to him. And opening his mouth he was teaching them saying: "Blessed are the poor in spirit, for theirs is the kingdom of heaven."

Key verse: *"Blessed are the poor in spirit, for theirs is the kingdom of heaven."* (Matt 5:3)

The popular 2005 movie *Batman Begins* details Bruce Wayne's transformation into the superhero Batman. One of the most thought provoking scenes occurs when Batman has just rescued his friend Rachelle Dawes from danger. As Batman sits perched on top of the ledge in heroic pose, Rachelle pleads "At least tell me your name." Batman then gives the classic response: "It's not who I am underneath, but what I *do* that defines me." After saying that, Batman turns and dramatically leaps from the ledge and glides away. Batman was suggesting that his true identity behind the mask was unimportant; rather, his public heroic actions were what really mattered.

In the mythical world of superheroes and secret identities, this idea makes perfect sense; it seems reasonable to have private lives that are very different from our public lives. In the biblical sense, however, *who* we are underneath is more important than *what* we do. Rather, *who* we are defines *what* we do and *why* we do it. God is not impressed with our public persona and outside reputation. Many Old Testament passages reveal the fact that God looks beyond the external and looks at the heart of men and women (see 1 Sam. 16:7; Prov. 16:2). Jesus, therefore, placed greater emphasis on "who we are in secret" instead of "what we are accomplishing in public".

Jesus begins the sermon with a series of beatitudes (blessed sayings); the very first blessing refers to a type of person who is blessed because they are "poor in spirit". The phrase "poor in spirit" refers to an *internal* quality; it describes a person who is conscious of their spiritual need. The location "in spirit" makes it clear that this is not about those who are poor financially, but rather those who recognize their total dependence on God; they sincerely understand that all things come from Him. In spite of intelligence, financial success, academic success, or physical giftedness, the person who is poor in spirit realizes that God gives gifts as He pleases and that we are all dependent on His grace. This dependence becomes a healthy antidote to the pride, arrogance, and the self-righteousness that we can develop because of our fallen nature. Being "poor in spirit" is a trademark of being a citizen in the kingdom of heaven. Therefore, this first beatitude sets the stage for the remaining beatitudes and the rest of the sermon. *Who* we are in secret is prior to *what* we do in public.

Reflection: *"Have you considered what it means to be poor in spirit? Is it possible to be poor in spirit and rich financially? Do you consider yourself poor in spirit? Why or why not?"*

"Having a Sober View of Life"

(Matthew 5:4 – 6)

Blessed are those who mourn, for they will be comforted.
Blessed are the humble for they will inherit the earth.
Blessed are those hungering and thirsting[1] for righteousness[2]
for they will be satisfied.

---

[1] The verbs translated "hungering and thirsting" describe the *manner* in which a person goes after righteousness.

[2] The word translated as righteousness has the direct object attached (literally: *the* righteousness). This likely indicates that *the* righteousness of God is in mind and not self-righteousness or human defined righteousness.

Key verse: *"Blessed are those who mourn, for they will be comforted."* (Matt 5:4)

I have heard some people suggest that "those who mourn" in Matt 5:4 refer to those who are mourning because of personal sin. Others look at the verse as simply referring to the normal sorrows of life. Either way, it is safe to assume that those who mourn are those who have hearts of flesh and understand the fallen state of this world. If we allow our hearts to be tender enough to respond to the needs around us, we will mourn. We mourn as we live in an imperfect world filled with sorrows, tragedies and sin. We mourn as we ourselves experience disappointments and adversity. But we do not mourn without hope. Jesus promises that there will be comfort. These same people are humble in heart and Jesus promises them an inheritance. As they hunger and thirst for the true righteousness that only God can provide, they are given a promise that they will be satisfied.

Those who are members of the kingdom of heaven have a sober view of life in this world. One of the things that make the bible so relatable is the fact that it contains every aspect of the human experience. Practically every type of sorrow, tragedy, and sin is shown at some point throughout the biblical narrative: murder, torture, rape, war, tragic accidents, sickness, unexpected death, etc. At the same time every type of joy is also experienced. I believe this highlights the authenticity of the bible. In the midst of it all, there stands a loving God who seeks to redeem His lost creation. Therefore, we celebrate joyous occasions and enjoy the good pleasures in life such as family, friends, good food, or a good movie. But we also understand that we will experience hardships and trials and suffer the loss of both people and things. Neither suffering nor success is permanent in this world. Therefore, our hope should not be in acquiring earthly goods or seeking to live the most comfortable life possible. Instead, we look forward to a heavenly country in which righteousness dwells (Heb. 11:16). There, we will be completely satisfied.

Prayer: *"Lord, there are things in this life that I really enjoy, like collecting dolls, fish and plants. Help me to put some of those efforts elsewhere… places that I can be a help towards people for your Name's sake. Lord, help me to have a sober view of life. Amen."*

Reflection: *"What is it that gives you hope in the midst of a world filled with tragedies and evil?"*

DAY 3

"Having the Right Motives"

(Matthew 5:7 – 9)

Blessed are the merciful, for they will receive mercy. Blessed are those who are pure in heart[3], for they will see God. Blessed are the peacemakers for they will be called children of God.[4]

---

[3] Greek dative of sphere; shows that the person is pure in their inmost being: in their heart (καρδία).

[4] The context indicates that υἱός (literally "sons") is being used in the wider sense than male offspring. I've translated as "children of God" instead of "sons of God".

Key verse: *"Blessed are those who are pure in heart, for they will see God."* (Matt 5:8)

It is possible for a person to do the right things for the wrong reasons. While *people* may be satisfied that the right deed was done, *God* also looks at the motives behind what was done. Many of the Old Testament proverbs touch on the importance of keeping a pure heart. Proverbs 4:23 mentions the importance of guarding our hearts because from it flows the *rivers* of our lives. Proverbs 21:2 mentions that God also looks inward at our hearts and weights (tests) it. There should always be two sets of eyes on our hearts examining it for purity and health: God's eyes and our eyes.

These next three beatitudes in the sermon mention the blessedness of those who are merciful, pure in heart, and makers of peace. The commonality of these three attributes is that they touch on how we are configured internally. It is possible for someone not inclined to have mercy to show mercy in a given situation. But being described as merciful, pictures someone with a heart of mercy; it is their nature to forgive, encourage and uplift others. The guarantee that they will receive mercy could be seen as divine passive (they will receive mercy from God), or it could simply highlight the fact that we reap what we sow.

The phrase "pure in heart" describes those that are free of deceit and sinful motives. They are told that they will get to see God. We will *all* see Him one day, but the blessedness here indicates that this is getting to see God favorably instead of in judgment. Those that are pure in heart and merciful seek to bring peace to both people and situations. Jesus declares that these people are the "children of God."

Prayer: "Lord, help me to have the right motives in everything that I do. I desire to be pleasing in your sight. Amen."

Reflection: "How often do you think about the reason WHY you do certain things?"

DAY 4

"Enduring Hardships as Followers of Christ"

(Matthew 5:10 – 12)

———•‖▸————————————————————◂‖•———

Blessed are those who have received persecution[5] because of righteousness for theirs is the kingdom of heaven. Blessed are you when [people] insult you and persecute and say all kinds of evil against you falsely [and] because of me. Rejoice and be exceedingly glad,

---

[5] The use of the Greek perfect tense may indicate a complete and ongoing persecution that the righteous are recipients of. The NASB is one of the few versions that translate the perfect (have received) tense instead of as a past (received) or present (receive) tense.

for your reward is great in heaven. For in this manner they persecuted the prophets before you.

Key verse: *"Rejoice and be exceedingly glad, for your reward is great in heaven. For in this manner they persecuted the prophets before you."* (Matt 5:12)

The rise to power and conversion of Constantine the Great was a remarkable change in both Christian history and world history. In the decade prior, Christians endured what is now known as The Great Persecution (303 – 313 AD)[6]. During this time, followers of Christ were thrown to lions for public entertainment in the coliseum. Christian documents were searched out and burned and a conscious effort was made to wipe Christianity from the face of the earth. Those that dared to become followers of Christ clearly understood the cost and potential dangers of that commitment.

A little over a decade later (324 A.D), the highest

---

[6] This was during the reign of Diocletian and was most likely instigated by his assistant Galerius who hated Christians and did not understand their faith in worshipping a crucified dead man (as he saw it). See Eusebius, *The Church History*, Translation and Commentary by Paul L. Maier, (Grand Rapids, Michigan: Kregel Publications, 2007)

official in the Roman government (now sole emperor), was a follower of Christ. Eventually, Christianity became the primary religion of the Roman Empire. Saints went from worshipping in basements to having large cathedrals built by the government. Bishops went from working bi-vocationally to receiving a government salary. The same government that crucified Christ began paying for mission trips. Those that lived through The Great Persecution must have been amazed.

On the surface this may appear to be a wonderful blessing with no downside. However, historians have long since noticed the direction the church has taken since then. In this new atmosphere of comfort, many Christians became more focused on things that are not essential to the Christian faith: the size and the beauty of church buildings, paid salaries, houses, church rank and titles, and public status. This trend continues in many parts of the Church today.

Instead of promising us riches and comfort, Jesus teaches us that those that practice righteousness will endure persecution. Those of us who are members of the kingdom of heaven will come into conflict with those who are in love with the things of this world. There is the chance that we can be insulted, persecuted, and spoken evil against because of our allegiance to Christ. We should definitely note that Jesus mentions that this evil should be spoken against us *falsely* and because of Him. If evil can be spoken against us in truth, then there is no blessing promised; in that case people are simply pointing out our hypocrisy. But when we are following Christ and doing His will, we rejoice in hardships, trials and persecution knowing that we have a greater reward in heaven.

Prayer: "Lord, help. That is much easier said than actually done. In times of trials I have wondered what have I done to deserve this or that. It is hard to imagine a great reward in heaven when experiencing trouble on earth. Help Lord."

Reflection: "During the Great Persecution, many Christians denied Christ under the threat of death. Later, when the persecution was over, they repented and reaffirmed Christ as Lord. What types of persecution are we willing to endure for Christ's sake? Or, do we deny Christ under social pressure?

"Representatives of Christ to a Fallen World"

(Matthew 5:13 – 16)

You are the salt of the earth. But if the salt becomes tasteless, how will it be made salty? It is useful for nothing except being thrown out to be trampled underfoot by men. You are the light of the world. A city located on a mountain cannot be hidden. Neither do people light a lamp and place it under the basket but on the lampstand and it gives light to those in the house. In this manner, your light must shine[7] before men that they may see your good works and glorify your Father in heaven.

Key verse: *"In this manner, your light must shine before men so that they many see your good works and glorify your Father in heaven."* (Matt 5:16)

The Greek philosopher Socrates is quoted as having said, "The unexamined life is not worth living." There are, however, many of us who live rather comfortably and do not pause long enough to reflect on the things happening around us; we live in our own personal bubble. Those who stop to examine what is happening around them (locally and globally) and what has happened historically, understand that we live a world that is filled with suffering, atrocities, hate, war, sickness and death. Furthermore, we ourselves are prone to anger, jealousy,

---

[7] The verb "shine" is in the Greek 3rd person singular imperative. Most English translations read: "let your light shine". Since English does not have a 3rd person imperative, it is hard to capture the thought. The word "let", while a good translation, can be taken too lightly with the imperative. In many cases, I think the word "must" better captures the force of the Greek 3rd person imperative.

pride, and lust. Because of God's common grace, there is some good in the world around us, but the world can rightly be classified as "fallen". It groans in pain as it eagerly awaits redemption (*Romans 8:22*).

Many have sought to answer the problems of mankind away from God and outside of Christ. Some look for answers financially thinking that money can solve our problem. Others look to the schools thinking that more education can solve our problem. Still others look to psychology and the behavioral and social sciences thinking that maybe there is a gene or a trait that can be extracted and analyzed to find an answer to the problems of evil and suffering. Jesus, however, gives a different diagnosis: the world has been darkened by sin and needs light. In this portion of the sermon he gives two analogies to describe his followers: salt and light. Salt is used to add flavor and to preserve. Jesus describes His followers as the salt of the earth. Our presence on earth should add the flavor of Christ to our work environment, neighborhoods, and communities. Jesus also describes His followers as the "light of the world". As followers of Christ, our lives should illuminate the way to genuine life that is only found in Christ (*John 14:6*).

In the midst of this, Jesus warns against salt becoming tasteless and light being hid under a basket.

Our light should not be locked away safe and secure in the sanctuary away from a world that needs it. Neither should our salt be corrupted and made tasteless by living a life stained by sin and hypocrisy. Instead, we should go out into the world and represent Christ in the various contexts in which He has placed us.

Prayer: *"Amen. Lord, help me to find where you want to use me. Perhaps I am already in that place."*

Reflection: *"In what ways do you make an impact as a follower of Christ? Does your relationship with Christ have an impact on your job? In your relationships and friendships?*

DAY 6

"God Does Not Change"
(Matthew 5:17 – 19)

Do not think that I came to do away with the law or the prophets; I did not come to do away with but to fulfill. For truly I say to you, until heaven and earth pass away, one iota or one stroke will never pass away from the law until all is accomplished. Therefore, whosoever sets aside one of the least of these commandments and teaches people likewise will be called least in the kingdom of heaven; whoever does these commandments and teaches others will be called great in the kingdom of heaven.

Key verse: *"Do not think that I came to do away with the law or prophets; I did not come to do away with but to fulfill."* (Matt 5:17)

I have actually heard Christians say that they do not believe that pastors should preach from the Old Testament because the New Testament does away with the old. It is as if they believe that the Old Testament no longer applies. However, a more accurate statement would be that the New Testament fulfills and grows from the old. Before going forward in His sermon, Jesus pauses to inform his listeners that what He is saying does not do away with what has already been written. The people in Jesus' day quoted and lived by the Old Testament. Even the smallest commandment that God had given was not to be overlooked.

Many themes explicitly mentioned in the Old Testament are clearly implied in the New Testament. We would do well to keep this in mind as we read and apply it. One major Old Testament theme is the holiness and sacredness of God. This is dramatically illustrated in the numerous ceremonial procedures and washings for the priests in the execution of their duties. God's same standard of holiness that was established in the law is not lowered in the New Testament. However, we can sometimes lose sight of this in the New Testament Church and treat the things of God with less reverence than is required.

Another theme is the fear of the Lord (*Job 28:28; 2 Chr. 19:9; Psalm 111:10; Prov. 1:7*). To say it plainly, God is dangerous. I have noticed that many intercessory prayers that are offered for people living a life of sin focus on God protecting those sinful persons from Satan and preserving them for salvation. However, the Scriptures make it plain that intercessors stand in the gap between the wayward sinner and God's judgment (*Ezek. 22:30*). This is not unlike Moses interceding for Israel (*Ex 32:11 – 14*) or Abraham for Sodom and Gomorrah (*Gen 18:23 – 33*). God's righteous judgment is the primary threat against sinners, not Satan.

God is holy and His sacred word still stands. We should make sure that we are familiar with God's entire word: both the Old and New Testaments. We should be careful to read and apply God's *entire* word as the whole canon of Scripture contains what is needed for our lives.

Reflection: *"Some people believe that the God of the Old Testament cannot possibly be the same God of the New Testament. They say that the love we see in Jesus we do not see from God in the Old Testament. What would be your response to such people?"*

DAY 7

"Superficial Religion Does Not Cut It"
(Matthew 5:20 – 28)

For I say to you that if your righteousness does not exceed greater than the scribes and Pharisees you will never enter the kingdom of heaven! You heard that it was said to those of old "Do not murder" for whoever murders is liable to judgment. But I say to you that everyone who becomes angry with his brother is liable to judgment and whoever says to his brother "empty headed fool" is liable to the council and whoever says "moron" is liable to the hell of fire. Therefore, if you present your gift on the altar and you remember that your brother has something against you, leave your gift there in front of the altar and go first make peace with your brother and then come and present your gift. Become friends with your opponent quickly while you are with him on the way so that he may not hand you over to the judge and the judge to the guard and you will be thrown into prison. Truly I say to you, you will not get out from there until you have paid the last penny! You heard that it was said, "You will not commit adultery." But I say to you that everyone who looks at a woman to lust for her, already committed adultery with her in his heart.

Key verse: *"For I say to you that if your righteousness does not exceed greater than the scribes and Pharisees you will never enter the kingdom of heaven."* (Matt 5:20)

In Jesus' day, the scribes and Pharisees were the interpreters and teachers of the law. As the community and religious leaders of Israel, they were experts of the Old Testament law and taught the people God's word. However, they missed the heart of God's commandments and only stressed external conformance to it. At some point they became self-deceived and were obsessed with their status and appearance among each other and before the people. Both Jesus and John the Baptist (Matt 3:7 – 12) called them out for their hypocrisy. Here, Jesus emphatically states that unless our righteousness exceeds the scribes and Pharisees we will *never* enter the kingdom of heaven. The word "never" is really an emphatic negation in the original Greek; in English it would come across as a double negative. It could perhaps be paraphrased as "you will never *ever* enter into the kingdom of heaven". This places serious stress on how unacceptable superficial righteousness is before Almighty God.

In the next few verses, Jesus provides several examples that expose superficial righteousness and reveal it as being insufficient. First, Jesus compares the act of murder with anger and name calling. They both stem from the same internal problem. He goes on to illustrate the inappropriateness of a person coming to worship (bringing a gift to the altar), while having hatred with his fellow Christian (brother). Jesus suggests that the act of worship should be stopped until the brotherly conflict is resolved! We cannot feign worship while allowing animosity to be present within the congregation.

Jesus continues with our treatment of people outside the church (an opponent at law). The Christian should have a good reputation even with those who are not yet followers of Christ. Jesus guarantees that we will not get preferential treatment if we wrong someone who is not a Christian; we will pay every penny for what we have done to those outside the church.

Finally, Jesus touches on the aspect of sexual sin. The Pharisees taught the people that as long as they did not commit sexual immorality they were not guilty of sin. Jesus goes into the motives of the heart; if we look with lustful intent, we are already guilty in the eyesight of God. This statement would make pornography and live nude "entertainment" forms of sexual sin.

Prayer: *"Lord Jesus, I want to be right externally as well as internally. I've got to see Jesus! Help me Lord as I strive for holiness in your sight. Amen."*

Reflection: *"Consider that Jesus says that we should stop worship until brotherly conflict is resolved. Have you ever tried to worship God while holding a grudge against someone? How was that worship experience?*

"Dealing with Internal Temptations to Sin"
(Matthew 5:29 – 30)

And if your right eye causes you to sin, cut it off and throw it from you; for it is better for you that you lose one of your parts and not your whole body be thrown into hell. And if your right hand causes you to sin, cut it off and throw it from you; for it is better for you that you lose one of your parts and not your whole body to go into hell.

Key verse: *"And if your right hand causes you to sin, cut it off and throw it from you..."* (Matt 5:30a)

After listening to Jesus talk about the dangers of superficial righteousness, it would have been natural for his listeners to think about the genuine temptations to sin that we all have. We *are* prone to anger, pride, and various lusts. We *are* tempted to talk about people who have wronged us and call them names. We *are* tempted to ignore those who are upset with us and go on our way without reconciliation. How do we deal with our internal parts that drive us toward sin?

Jesus does not answer that question here. The response that Jesus gives focuses more on the dangers of not taking these internal threats seriously. Jesus uses the violent imagery of dismemberment (cutting off limbs, plucking out eyes) to show that our breaking with sin may be painful. However, this breaking is lifesaving. Similar to a person that must lose a limb to stop a growing cancer and save his or her life, sin must be eradicated to save our souls from hell. Anything that leads us into sin needs to be cut off and thrown as far away from us as possible. If we recognize that we have a weakness in a certain area, then we need to be honest with ourselves and stay away from the people, situations, or things that can become a stumbling block into sin.

Jesus does not go into detail here concerning our help to guard against the attractive force of sin. However, it is taught later in Scripture that we have help from the Holy Spirit who gives us strength to live according to God's will (*Rom 8:1 – 5*). Therefore, let us walk in the Spirit and take serious the temptations into sin.

Prayer: *"Lord, thank You for Your Holy Spirit that gives me the strength to live in the world but not of it. Amen."*

Reflection: *"Have you ever had to remove certain "nouns" (people, places, things) from your life to avoid sin? Was it difficult? What prompted you to make such a change?"*

"The Beauty of the Marriage Covenant"
(Matthew 5:31 – 32) / (Matthew 19:3 – 12)

And it has been said, "Whoever divorces his wife, he must give her a written notice of divorce". But I say to you that everyone who divorces his wife, except for sexual immorality, makes her commit adultery and whoever marries a woman having been divorced commits adultery.

---

[8] See Appendix A for a translation of Matt. 19:3-12

Key verse: "*So then they are no longer two but one flesh. Therefore, what God joined together a man must not separate*" (Matt 19:6)

The statement that Jesus makes in Matthew 5:31 – 32 has to be understood in its social and historical context. In Jesus' day, most Jewish women did not have the same civil rights as their husbands who could divorce them at any time and for any reason. The only thing a man needed was a written document and then he could literally *release* (*apolyō*)[9] his wife. The rationale was based on the interpretation of Deut. 24:1: *If a man finds a woman and marries her, and it happens that she finds no favor in his eyes because he has found something indecent in her, [then] he [can] write her a letter of divorce, put it in her hand, and send her from his house.* Some Rabbis taught that "something indecent" meant some form of gross immoral failure. However, many taught that it was determined by the husband; if the husband considered something indecent then it was. Therefore, in practice, the husband could divorce his wife for *any* reason he saw fit. An event that occurs in Matthew

---

[9] Literally "release" or "set free". In the context of marriage, the word is translated into English as divorce.

chapter 19:3 – 12 is seen in light of this historical and cultural understanding; the phrase in Matt. 5:31-32 is better understood in light of the more complete teaching that Jesus gives there.

In Matthew chapter 19, the Pharisees try to test Jesus by asking him the loaded question, *"It is lawful for a man to divorce his wife for any reason?"*[10] This was a trick question to test Jesus' understanding of Old Testament law. If Jesus answers *"No, it is not lawful"*, he may lose some of his male followers as they loved having this option and considered it clear OT teaching. If he answers *"Yes, it is lawful"*, he may lose most of his female followers who desperately wanted the social climate to change. This was an attempt to ruin Jesus' credibility as a teacher and divide his following. How will Jesus answer?

Instead of answering directly, Jesus goes back to the original beauty of God's design of the marriage relationship. To show that a woman is not a second-class citizen, he first mentions that in the beginning God made them male *and* female. *Both* are made in the image of God and have inherent self-worth. Jesus is actually referencing the poetic refrain of Genesis 1:27:

---

[10] Matt 19:3; my translation. See appendix A below.

36

> So, God created mankind in His own image, in the image of God he created him; male *and* female he created them.

Jesus then mentions how a man leaves his father and mother and is literally *glued*[11] to his wife. The verb translated as "glued" is in the passive voice indicating that neither the man nor the woman is the active agent applying the glue. A few verses later, Jesus reveals that God was the one applying the glue (...*what God has joined together*). A marriage joined together by God is strong indeed!

In the Old Testament, a father was the physical and spiritual covering[12] for his family which including his adult daughter until she was married. At that time, he would give her over to her husband and then the husband would become one with his wife and be the covering over that new family unit. I love how the traditional marriage ceremony models this great biblical

---

[11] *kollaō*. Literally means to be glued or fastened firmly together.
[12] By "physical covering", I mean protection. The father was to protect his family against physical harm and danger. The men would fight while the women and children stayed home. The father was also the spiritual covering; ultimately it was his responsibility to teach them God's word and make sure they understood the things of God (see Job 1:4-5; Prov. 15:5; Deut. 6:6-7). For a New Testament teaching see Eph. 6:4.

truth. The husband, having already left his father and mother, stands tall at the altar. No one can give him away because he is a man; he has already separated himself from his father and mother. Then the doors of the sanctuary open and the woman appears holding the hand of her father. The entire church stands. At that moment her father is still her spiritual and physical covering. After he walks her down the aisle, the clergyman ceremonially asks, "Who gives this woman to this man?" and the father answers, "I do". As the husband reaches out and takes the hand of his bride, the spiritual and physical covering is transferred from the father to him. He is glued to his wife. The two become one flesh.

After explaining to the Pharisees this original concept of marriage, Jesus states that while God allowed (through Moses) men to divorce their wives, this was not the original design. God did not create Adam and several "spares" in case things did not work out with the first wife. The trivial reasons that men gave for abandoning their wives were wicked in the eyesight of God. Unless their wives committed adultery, they did not have a legitimate reason to do what they were doing.[13] Marriage is a sacred covenant relationship that is established and sealed by God. It is to be honored as such.

---

[13] Our culture is vastly different than the first century Jewish culture in which Jesus lived and taught. In our culture, divorce can be initiated by the man or the woman. I believe that serious issues such as domestic violence and child abuse may also be legitimate grounds for divorce. Some clergy disagree and believe that Jesus' statement of "sexual immorality" is the only legitimate grounds regardless of cultural context. A pastor friend of mine disagreed with me when I told him that I thought domestic violence can be grounds for divorce. He believed that adultery was the only biblical grounds due to Jesus' statement in Matthew 5:31-32. Given the context, I believe that Jesus' teaching on divorce can be understood as: "Divorce is only a valid option in serious violations of the marriage covenant (i.e. sexual immorality)". In Jesus' culture that was the only grounds for a *man* to evict his *wife*; Jesus was speaking out against men who were leaving their wives for trivial reasons. In our society, I would include domestic violence and child abuse as serious violations and grounds for a *wife* to serve papers to her abusive *husband*. The apostle Paul included abandonment as grounds for divorce (see 1 Corinthians 7:10-16; if the unbelieving spouse separates). For further study on the social and historical context of marriage and divorce, see David Instone-Brewer, *Divorce and Remarriage in the Bible: The Social and Literary Context* (Grand Rapids, Michigan: Wm. B. Eerdmans Publishing Co., 2002).

Reflection: "*Statistics show that divorce rates within the church are very similar to the rates outside the church. Why do you think that is so? How can we strengthen marriages and lower the divorce rate in the church?*"

DAY 10

"Being Careful with Words"

(Matthew 5:33 – 37)

Again, you heard that it was said to those of yesterday "you will not break a promise but will pay back your promise to the lord." But I say to you do not promise at all. Not by heaven, since it is the throne of God. Neither by the earth, since it is a footstool for his feet. Nor in Jerusalem, since it is the city of the great king. Neither swear by your head, since you cannot make one hair white or black. But your yes must be yes and your no must be no; anything more than these is from the evil one.

Key verse: "*But your yes must be yes and your no must be no; anything more than these is from the evil one*" (Matt 5:37)

It is believed by most scholars that the New Testament book of James was written by James the half-brother of Jesus. In the middle of this short epistle, James gives an extended discourse on the dangers of not watching our words (*James 3:1 – 12*). He suggests that the task of guarding our tongue is difficult and that the person who is disciplined enough to guard it is complete and capable of controlling every other urge in his or her body. According to James, it is almost second nature for most of us to speak first and think later.

In this portion of his sermon, Jesus begins to discuss the importance of how we use words. Specifically, he deals with the manner in which people made vows to validate that they would actually do what they said. The idea was that if they made a promise to the Lord, or swore by something great, then they were obligated to follow through with those words. Without a solemn vow to back up what was said, many people probably felt that it was optional to follow through.

Jesus teaches his listeners not to swear by anything since they do not have ultimate authority. We do not have authority over heaven to swear by it since it is the place of God's throne. Neither do we have authority over the earth to swear by it since it is God's footstool. We do not even have authority to swear by our own heads since our very lives are in God's hands and he even controls our hair color. Instead, we are to be people who think before we speak and follow through with what we say. Our yes should actually be yes. Interestingly, Jesus states that anything more that this is from the evil one who happens to be very crafty with words.

Prayer: *"Lord, help me to continue to watch what I say. Amen"*

Reflection: *"Have you ever noticed how some people use certain phrases to emphasize the truth of their words? Phrases such as: "Honest to God...", "No, seriously...", "In all honesty..." Do you feel the need to use phrases like these for people to believe what you say? Why or why not?*

"Learning to Defuse Heated Situations"

(Matthew 5:38 – 42)

You have heard that is was said "an eye in place of an eye" and "a tooth in place of a tooth" But I say to you, do not resist the evil one. But whoever hits you on your right check, turn to him the other also. And whoever desires to sue you and take your shirt, give to him also your garment. And whoever will force you to go one mile, go with him two. Give to the one asking and do not refuse the one desiring to borrow from you.

Key verse: "*You have heard that it was said 'An eye in place of an eye' and 'A tooth in place of a tooth.' But I say to you*

*to not oppose the one who is evil. But whoever hits you on
your right cheek, turn to him the other cheek also."* (Matt
5:38 – 39)

Many people have wrongly interpreted the Old
Testament phrase "An eye for an eye, and a tooth for
a tooth" as meaning that it used to be okay to seek out
vengeance.[14] However, when this Old Testament passage
is properly interpreted it reveals that the command was
given to prevent a situation from escalating. It is the
law of equal retribution. When we are hurt by others,
we have a tendency to want them to suffer *worse* than
what we have suffered. If you take one of my eyes, I may
want to take both of your eyes along with three teeth
and a limb…or maybe two. The command to limit my
response to one eye keeps things from escalating and
only allows for *equal* retribution.

After quoting this Old Testament phrase, Jesus
raises the bar for his followers. Instead of allowing
us to return equal measure, Jesus teaches us to *defuse*
heated situations. After informing us not to oppose an
evil person, Jesus follows with three difficult examples

[14] The passage is Exodus 21:24 and actually refers to procedures
to take if a pregnant woman is injured by the carelessness of
others.

to illustrate his point. The first is the one that most Christians have had a hard time accepting. Jesus says that if a person smacks you on the right side of your face, turn and allow them the other side as well. Some interpret this verse as a literal slap and believe Christians have to allow people to slap them. However, I believe that Jesus is using hyperbole (as he does a few times in this sermon).[15] The slap on the cheek should be seen as some sort of gross insult or form of disrespect. The point is to not respond in kind and to be willing to endure such treatment again.

The other two examples teach how the Christian is to respond in active kindness to an aggressive person. The giving away of a garment and the walking of a few miles speaks of maturity and patience. Jesus' words here are very challenging. Should Christians be passive doormats for aggressive people to walk over? I would say no. Instead of allowing equal retribution (a return slap perhaps?), Jesus wants us to defuse the heated situation as much as possible. As opposed to thinking that we are *passively* receiving abuse, we are to be *actively* obedient to God. Similarly, Jesus did not passively receive mistreatment at the cross, instead He

---

[15] See Matt. 5:29 above. Jesus does not mean to literally cut off your hand and pluck out your eye. He is using hyperbole to grab attention make emphasis.

actively sought the prize that was in front of Him: *"Who for the joy standing in front of Him, endured the cross, thinking nothing of the shame, and has sat down at the right hand of God." Hebrews 12:2b.*

Reflection: *"Has an unbeliever (or Christian) ever challenged you on the 'turn-the-other' cheek passage? What was your response? How do you respond when someone has insulted or disrespected you?*

"A New Understanding of Love"

(Matthew 5:43 – 48)

You heard that it was said love your neighbor and hate your enemy. But I say to you: love your enemies and pray on behalf of those who are persecuting you. So that you may become children of your father who is in heaven, because he causes his sun to rise on the evil and the good, and he sends rain on the righteous and the unrighteous. For if you love those loving you, what reward do you have? Don't also the tax-collectors do the same? And if you greet your brothers only, what more have you done? Don't also the foreigners do the same?

Therefore, you shall be perfect as your heavenly father is perfect.

Key verse: *"But I say to you: love your enemies and pray on behalf of those who are persecuting you.* (Matt 5:44)

How fitting that Jesus goes from "turn-the-other-cheek" to talking about loving our enemies. When most people think of love, they think of either romance, friendship, or some sort of family relationship. The Greeks had a different word for each of these types of love. The romantic, passionate type of love that *should* exist within the marriage relationship is called *eros*, which is the root for the English word "erotic". The word for the love that describes the bond between two close friends is called *phileo;* the city of Philadelphia is named from the Greek "brotherly love". The word for love that was used to describe the familial bond between family members is called *storge*. Neither of these words is used to describe the type of love that God has for us and that we are commanded to have for others. The word used for that love, and the one that Jesus commands, is called *agape*. It refers to love that is unconditional.

Many have sought to provide a definition that best

describes the word *agape* in its New Testament usage. The best definition that I have heard states that agape is *"the unconditional, purely motivated, and active pursuit of its object's best interest."* Perhaps when Christians hear the command: "love your enemies" they usually begin to think one of the other types of love. Needless to say, those categories of love do not fit the context of dealing with an enemy. Loving our enemy has nothing to do with friendship, family ties, partnership, or passionate feelings. As shown in the verses immediately preceding, loving our enemies refers to *how we respond* to them. We are to pray for them and actively look out for their best interests from a pure heart. When we begin to love our enemies, we become more like God who loved us while we were His enemies (*Rom 5:8*).

Reflection: *"How does the definition of agape help make clear the concept of loving our enemies?"*

DAY 13

"Who is Your Audience?"

(Matthew 6:1 – 18)

And you make certain to not do your righteous deeds before people to be seen by them. Otherwise you have no reward with your father in heaven. Therefore, whenever you do almsgiving, do not sound a trumpet before you, just as the hypocrites do in the synagogues and in the streets so that they may be praised by people. Truly I say to you, they are receiving their reward. But when you give alms, do not let your left hand know what your right hand is doing. So that your almsgiving may be in secret and your father seeing in secret will pay back to you. And when you pray, do not be as the hypocrites because they love to stand praying in the synagogues and the corners of streets so that they might be made known to people. Truly I say to you they are receiving their reward in full. But when you pray, enter your private room and shut your door. Pray to your father in secret and your father seeing in secret will reward you. And while praying do not use many words like the foreigners for they think that because of their many words they will be heard. Therefore, do not be similar to them; for your Father knows what you have need of before you ask him. Therefore, in this manner you pray: Our Father who is in heaven, let your name be made holy; let your kingdom come, let your will be done on earth just as it is in heaven. Give us our necessary bread for today. And forgive us our wrong doing even as we forgive those who have wronged us. And do not bring us into temptation but deliver us from the evil one. For if you forgive people their misdeeds, your heavenly father will forgive you. But if you do not forgive people, neither will your father forgive your misdeeds. And when you fast, do not be like the hypocrites with sad countenances. For they make their faces unsightly so that they may appear fasting to people. Truly I say to you, they are receiving their reward in full. But when you fast, anoint your head and wash your face so that you do not appear fasting to people but rather to your father in secret and your father seeing in secret will reward you.

Key verse: *"And when you pray, do not be as the hypocrites for they love to stand praying in the synagogues and the corners of streets so that they might be made known to people. Truly I say to you they are receiving their reward in full."* (Matt 6:5)

In many charismatic churches, it is common for the listeners to respond with verbal shouts during the sermon. People will shout "Amen!" or "You preaching!" or "Say it Pastor!" to let the preacher know they are in agreement with what has been said. Some preachers expect this and believe something is terribly wrong if they are not receiving it. In fact, I have seen some actually pause to rebuke the congregation for not responding to what they feel is good preaching. Sometimes this extends to the public prayers that are offered during the worship service. Many people lead public prayer with a certain rhythm and lively passion. As people shout in agreement with the person praying, there is the temptation for the person praying to wax long and dramatic to hear more shouts. (Some people refer to this as "preaching the prayer"). If the person is not careful, they will find themselves no longer talking to God. Instead they are attempting to stir-up those who are listening.

This long section is almost a sermon within the sermon. Jesus makes his main idea in verse one: *"Do not do righteous deeds to be seen by others"*. He then follows with three examples of righteous deeds that should not be done to impress others: giving to the poor, praying, and fasting. The Pharisees were guilty of all three. Jesus openly called them hypocrites and informed his followers to not be like them. The Pharisees wanted to impress people by how much money they gave; they wanted to appear generous in the eyes of the masses. They prayed long prayers in the synagogues and street corners to give the appearance of righteousness. They wanted people to see how often they fasted so that people would be impressed with their commitment to holiness. Jesus mentioned that the Pharisees were already "receiving" their reward from the masses. The verb translated "receiving" is in the present tense to dramatically show that each pretentious act was actually *being* rewarded by the eyes of the people. God was not the intended audience, the people were.

Our devotion to God is not to be an ostentatious act. They are to be done in secret as sincere acts of worship and obedience. Giving is to be done quietly with the right motive. Prayers are to be offered *to God* seeking an audience with Him. We are to fast as an act of devotion to God in secret. When done in this manner, Jesus promises that we will receive our reward from heaven.

Prayer: *"Lord, help me to continue to do good for your eyes and not to impress people. Amen."*

Reflection: *"How do you give to people, privately or publicly? Do you feel the need to let others know how much you gave, how often you pray, or how many people you've helped? Why?*

DAY 14

"Where is Your Treasure?"
(Matthew 6:19 – 24)

Do not store for yourself treasures on the earth, where moth and rust ruin and where thieves dig through and steal. But store for yourself treasures in heaven where neither moth nor rust ruin and where thieves do not dig through neither steal. For where your treasure is, there your heart will be also. The lamp of the body is the eye. Therefore, if your eye is good your entire body will be full of light. But if your eye is evil, your entire body will be full of darkness. Therefore, if the light in you is darkness, how great is the darkness. No one is able to serve two lords. For either he will detest one and love the other or he will be loyal to one and despise the other. You cannot serve God and money.

Key verse: *"For where your treasure is, there your heart will be also."* (Matt 6:21)

A rapper once released an album entitled "Get Rich or Die Trying". The album was a mega hit and sold millions. The title of album describes the approach to life that many people have. The primary goal of many is to live the best life now by making the highest salary, accumulating the most wealth, and living the most comfortable life possible. Since their eyes are never satisfied (*Prov. 27:19*), they are always seeking for more.

In this portion of the sermon, Jesus warns about accumulating treasures here on earth. The material blessings that we receive on earth are not only uncertain, but they can never fully satisfy (*see 1 Tim 6:17*). Instead, Jesus teaches that we are to store up more permanent treasures in heaven. This exhortation reminds us that there is a life after this one. The things we do here on earth have ramifications for what happens next.

The affections of our heart determine the way we see all of life. We all wear an invisible pair of glasses that affects *how* we see and *what* we see in any given situation. Jesus explains that if our hearts are selfish and centered on gain (accumulating treasures on earth), then our eyes become evil and we see life through the lens of self-gain, self-gratification and greed. But if our hearts are pure and seeking to please God, then our eyes become good and everything is seen through the lens of serving God and helping others.[16] Hence, two people can view the exact same situation with two totally different perspectives. Jesus makes it clear that if our hearts and treasures are here on earth, we cannot serve God.

Prayer: *"Lord, help me here. I want money, lots of it… millions of it, if I can get it. But not just for me and my family, but to help people in need. Money is not evil. The*

---

[16] This also reminds me of a statement Paul said in his letter to Titus: *"To the pure, all things are pure, but to the defiled and unbelieving nothing is pure; but both their minds and their consciences are defiled"* (Titus 1:15). Here Paul is talking about a subset of Jewish teachers (Cretans) who "turn away from the truth" and "profess to know God" but "deny Him their works". Notice the distinction between *"all things are pure"* and *"nothing is pure"*. Here, I believe Paul has in mind a similar concept of "invisible glasses". The Cretans could never see truth or accept it because their heart condition blinded them; they could not see good or purity in anything.

love of it is. I want to do more in the world and having more money can make that happen."

Reflection: *"How often do we hear sermons about heaven? How often do you think about heaven?*

DAY 15

"Trusting God to Meet our Needs"
(Matthew 6:25 – 34)

Because of this I say to you do not worry about your life, what you will eat or drink or your body, what you will wear. Is not life more than food and the body more than clothing? Look to the birds of the air for they do not sow nor reap. They neither gather into barns and your heavenly father provides them with food. Are not you worth much more than them? And which of you from your worrying is able to add one hour to his life? And why are you worrying about clothing? Consider the flowers of the field how they grow and do not work hard nor spin. And I say to you that not even Solomon in all his glory was clothed as one of these. Therefore, if God so clothes the grass of the field being here today and thrown into the fire tomorrow, will not much more he clothe you, you of little faith? Therefore, do not be anxious saying what we shall eat or what we shall drink or what we shall wear; for all these the foreigners seek after. For your heavenly father knows that you need all of these things. But seek first the kingdom of God and his righteousness and all these things will be added to you. Therefore, do not be anxious about tomorrow, for tomorrow will look out for itself. Sufficient for the day is its own evil.

Key verse: *"But seek first the kingdom of God and His righteousness and all these things will be added to you."* (Matt 6:33)

One of the motivating factors that drive people to store up wealth is the fear of not having enough. If we have plenty of money in the bank and decent medical insurance, home owner's insurance, car insurance, life insurance, and the like, we feel more secure about the uncertainties of life. However, after exhorting us to serve God and store up treasures in heaven, Jesus teaches us not to be anxious about our own natural needs. He promises us that if God takes care of the animals and nature, God will certainly take care of us. Being released from this anxiety, our primary efforts are to seek God's kingdom here on earth.

It is important to note here that Jesus does not have in mind a carefree attitude towards life. Being carefree and irresponsible is not the same thing as having faith. We should be wise stewards over what God has blessed us with, work hard and plan ahead. One wise preacher noted that although God *does* provide for the birds of the air (verse 26), the birds must leave their nests and seek and gather what has been set aside for them; God honors and rewards hard work. Instead, what Jesus is teaching against is the excessive worrying that shows a lack of faith and trust in God. Jesus does not promise excessive riches when we trust God (our hearts should not be set on that anyway), but rather God will take care of our natural needs.

Reflection: *"I'm writing this day's reflection in late March 2020. We are in the midst of the global Coronavirus pandemic. This quick spread of the virus has caused many to worry. Many people are questioning God. How do you trust God to meet your needs when the future seems uncertain?"*

DAY 16

"Qualified Counselors"
(Matthew 7:1 – 6)

Do not judge so that you may not be judged. For in whatever judgment you judge, you will be judged; and in whatever measure you measure out it will be measured to you. And why do you see the speck in the eye of your brother and not consider the tree in your eye? Or how will you say to your brother "Let me remove the speck from your eye" and behold the tree in your eye! Hypocrite! First remove the tree from your eye and then you will see clearly to remove the speck from the eye of your brother. Do not give [what is] holy to dogs. Neither throw your pearls before pigs, so that they will not trample them under their feet and then turning they might tear you into pieces.

Key verse: *"First remove the tree from your eye and then you will see clearly to remove the speck from the eye of your brother"* (Matt 7:5)

Many people who are living with sinful habits take solace in quoting Matthew 7:1. They translate the second usage of the word "judge" as a *divine passive* meaning that God will judge people that point out their faults to them. However, the context of the passage is far from allowing that interpretation. The Scriptures clearly indicate that we are to be watchful over each other and lovingly point out the error of sinful ways (see *Matt. 18:15; James 5:19–20; 1 Cor. 5:9-13*). In this segment of the sermon, Jesus teaches on the *qualifications* for correcting others and to be *discerning* when trying to help others.

Verses one and two of Matthew 7 state the obvious: people automatically hold us to the same standard that we proclaim they should live by. We cannot preach what we are not living. If we are not living what we are proclaiming, then we are in worse condition than the people we are preaching to. In that case we become self-deceived and have a *tree* hanging out of our eye, whereas they only have a *speck*. Jesus' choice of words here is intentional and critical. He uses the word for a log or beam used in major construction as compared to a small speck of dust. Obviously, the tree must be removed before we can address the speck.

Then there are times when people do not want to hear the truth of our words. Jesus refers to this as giving what is holy to dogs or casting pearls before swine. The image is of someone receiving something good and precious and treating it like trash. After rejecting your words, Jesus says that they may "turn and tear you into pieces". Because of the content of the message, they may attack the messenger. In this situation, I believe we should pray for God to soften their heart and witness through our actions until an appropriate time comes to minister with words.

Reflection: "Have you ever tried to correct someone and then they point out similar faults in your life? Did you ever give good advice to a person only to have them respond in unexpected anger or hostility? How did you respond?

DAY 17

"It Is Not Without Effort"

(Matthew 7:7 – 12)

Ask and it will be given to you. Seek and you will find. Knock and it will be opened to you. For all those who ask receives, and the one who seeks finds, and for the one knocking it will be opened. Or which man is among you whose son asks him bread he will not give him a stone, [will he][17]? Or if he asks for a fish he will not give him a snake, [will he]? Therefore, if you being evil know to give good gifts to your children, how much

---

[17] The presence of the Greek particle μὴ indicates that the question is expecting a negative answer. Similar to the NASB, I have translated to make the baited question explicit.

more will your Father in heaven give good to those asking him? Therefore, everything that you desire that people do to you, in this manner you should do to them; for this is the law and the prophets.

Key verse: *"Ask and it will be given to you. Seek and you will find. Knock and it will be opened to you."* (Matt 7:7)

Once during a bible study, someone asked the minister who was leading the study, *"Why did Elijah have to pray so earnestly for God to send rain?"* He was referring to the narrative found in 1 Kings 18:41 – 46 where Elijah is persistently praying for God to end a drought and send rain. The rationale for the question was that God had already promised to send rain in verse one. Since God had already promised rain (40 verses earlier), then why require this exercise in persistence to receive the promise? The minister admitted that the bible did not give an explicit answer, but did offer a suggestion. His suggestion was that *"Maybe God enjoys spending time with us and building character in us instead of always answering quick prayers."* I believe that the minister was on to something.

In this portion of the sermon, Jesus encourages his listeners to be persistent in their pursuit of the promises of God. We are not to ask and sit back passively waiting for things to fall down from heaven. Instead, through prayerful discernment we are to keep our eyes open in expectation that God will bless us. As we wait for answers to specific prayers, we are actively seeking God and pursuing His purposes. Here Jesus refers to God as our "Father who is in heaven". A good father does not neglect the needs of his children. At the same time, a good father attempts to instill discipline and character in his children. We can expect both of these from a decent father on earth. Jesus teaches that we should expect it even more from our heavenly Father.

Reflection: "Have you ever seen a spoiled child? (For example: a child with no restrictions who was immediately granted everything he or she requested.) What type of character and personality do you think is being developed as these spoiled children grow into adulthood? What type of Christians would we be if God immediately gave us everything that we asked for?"

"The Path Less Traveled"

(Matthew 7:13 – 14)

Go in through the narrow game. Because wide [is] the gate and broad [is] the way leading into destruction and many are entering through it. For narrow [is] the gate and having been made difficult[18] is the way leading to life and they are few finding it.

---

[18] The verb translated "having been made difficult" is a perfect passive participle in the Greek. Some modern translations render the verb as an intransitive: "narrow (difficult) *is* the way". The perfect passive can also indicate that the requirements for entering the kingdom have been *purposely* set to demand a high level of surrender and sacrifice; I have translated in this manner.

Key verse: *"For narrow is the gate and having been made difficult is the way leading to life and they are few finding it."* (Matt 7:14)

Sometimes the path less traveled is the best route to take. There have been times when I have purposely taken the longer route and after arriving to my destination I learned that I avoided a traffic pileup. Jesus describes the gate to the path that leads to life as narrow and the gate to the path that leads to destruction as wide. Some focus on the narrowness of the gate to life and suggest that this represents Jesus as the only way to heaven. They believe that the broad gate is symbolic of every path of righteousness outside of Christ. Others focus on the few finding the path to life and suggest that this means that not many people will meet the requirements for heaven.

There is likely truth in both of these aspects. Elsewhere, Jesus declares Himself to be the only way to the Father (John 14:6); and already in the sermon He has warned against superficial righteousness (Matt 5:20), hypocrisy (Matt 6:2), and besetting sins (Matt 5:2) that can prevent us from entering into the kingdom of heaven. We should not be deceived into thinking that all roads lead to heaven and that truth is relative. By definition, truth excludes what is false; Jesus claimed to be *the* truth.[19] Neither should we take Jesus' warnings lightly and presuppose that superficial faith and "minor" habitual sins may be okay. In honesty and humility, we should constantly seek God in reflective prayer and ask him to reveal anything that may be offensive in us. The closing prayer of David in Psalm 139 expresses this notion wonderfully (Psalms 139:23 – 24).

Prayer: *"Amen. Lord, lead me!"*

Reflection: *"As an Air Force chaplain, from time to time I lead an ethics briefing with new officers. One of the questions I ask them is: What standard do you use to determine what is morally right or wrong? Often, some will suggest that right or wrong is not objective; rather, it based on what is accepted by the majority. Do you agree with this? Can what is accepted by the majority be wrong? Why or why not?*

---

[19] In addition, Jesus explained to Pontius Pilate that allegiance to Him determines if a person is on the side of truth or not (John 18:37). I think this is one of the most fascinating statements made by Jesus. The implication of Jesus' words is that any form of spirituality that does not have Him at the center is false.

DAY 19

"Got Fruit?"
(Matthew 7:15 – 20)

Watch out for false prophets who come to you in sheep's clothing but on the inside they are savage wolves. From their fruit you will know them. They don't gather grapes from thorn plants or figs from briars, do they? Thus, every good tree makes good fruit, but the bad tree makes evil fruit. A good tree [is] not able to make bad fruit; neither [is] a bad tree able to make good fruit. Every tree not making good fruit [is] chopped down and thrown into fire. Therefore, from their fruit you will know them.

Key verse: *"From their fruit you will know them. They don't gather grapes from thorn plants or figs from briars, do they?"* (Matt 7:16)

Many people come into ministry settings with impure motives. Some pretend to be followers of Christ in order to gain money, position or prestige. Others feign religiosity as they search for vulnerable Christian singles in an attempt to entice them into sexual immorality. Jesus labels such people as wolves in sheep's clothing. On the surface they pretend to be sheep, but on the inside, they are savage wolves. Jesus offers a rather simple test to discern sheep from wolves: by observing their fruit.

The next logical question is "How do we recognize fruit?" In the New Testament, the term *fruit* is used as a metaphor to describe character traits. As these traits "grow", they reveal the type of seed that has been planted. In Galatians 5, Paul distinguishes the works of the flesh against the *fruit* of the Spirit. Things such as sensuality, jealousy, idolatry, strife, and rivalry are compared to love, peace, kindness, self-control and gentleness. If we are not careful we can be distracted by the outward appearance of financial success, charisma, and popularity and miss the signs of rotten fruit. Many leaders are blatantly arrogant, proud, and flashy. Sadly, many who follow such leaders are sincerely mislead. Distracted by forms without substance, they only realize something is wrong after a major public scandal.

Jesus warns that every tree that bears bad fruit will be cut down. Therefore, followers of Christ should strive to grow good fruit. A sign of good spiritual vitality is that we are producing good spiritual fruit such as: maturity in speech, honesty, integrity, discipline, self-control, compassion, empathy, and knowledge and the understanding of God's word.

Reflection: "I have noticed that the truth of God can be distorted through word or through deed. There are some who teach false doctrine (heterodoxy), yet they perform some good deeds. On the other hand, there are those who teach sound doctrine (orthodoxy) while living sinful lives. Which do you think is more dangerous? How can the fruit of the Spirit help us to avoid these two errors?"

DAY 20

"Deceived Hypocrites"
(Matthew 7:21 – 23)

Not everyone saying to me "Lord, lord" will enter into the kingdom of heaven but the one doing the will of my Father in heaven. Many will say to me in that day "Lord, lord, did not we preach in your name and cast out demons in your name and do many miracles in your name?" And then I will say plainly to them that "I never knew you. Go away from me you lawbreakers!"

Key verse: *"And then I will say to them plainly that, 'I never knew you. Go away from me you lawbreakers!'"* (Matt 7:23)

It is possible for people to start believing their own lies. After playing a role for so long, they become locked into that role and are no longer honest with themselves. The Scriptures warn that sin can have this sort of effect on us. Hebrews 3:13 reads, "Rather, exhort each other every day, as it is called today, so that none of you may be hardened by the deceitfulness of sin." To be both deceived *and* hardened is to be in a dangerous state. If a person is deceived but has a soft and open heart, there is a chance they may accept correction. But if the heart becomes hardened, they will refuse correction and remain in that state.

In this section of the sermon, Jesus describes a day when many people will be surprised. Those who have done many good works in the name of the Lord will be told to depart from His presence. Then they will begin to question this judgment and bring up previous accomplishments. Although they will have done many things in ministry, Jesus calls them workers of *anomia*. This word can describe someone who has contempt for a law, or someone who violates the law through *ignorance* or *blatant disregard*. This suggests that in the midst of "successful" ministry, these people were breaking God's laws. Their ignorance, it appears, was not an excuse.

The fact that the lawbreakers are confused about Jesus' announcement shows they were deceived in their sin against God. Perhaps they got caught up in worldly metrics of success and ignored sin in their lives. Maybe they began to believe their own lies and confused financial success or popularity with God's favor. Or maybe, like Sampson (*Judges 13 – 16*), they convinced themselves that their giftedness allowed them to get away with habitual sin. Either way, Jesus says that He will make it very clear that he never knew them. It would be wise of us to constantly monitor ourselves to be sure that we are not deceived. The exhortation from Peter is well heeded: *"Therefore, brothers, be more earnest to make your calling and election sure. For if you do these things, you may never fall." 2 Peter 1:10.*[20]

Reflection: "Does this passage give you concern to pause and think about your salvation? How confident are you that you will not be one of the lawbreakers Jesus is referring to? How do you know?

---

[20] The "things" that Peter is referring to can be found in verses 5 – 7: moral excellence, knowledge, self-control, endurance, godliness, brotherly love (*philadelphia*), and Christian love (*agape*). Peter states that Christians have to "be earnest" about supplementing their faith with these things. This gives the impression that we have to make a conscious decision to obey the Holy Spirit in order for growth and improvement to take place. The alternative is to be a Christian that is ineffective and unfruitful (verse 8).

"A Strong Foundation"
(Matthew 7:24 – 29)

Therefore, all who hear these words of mine and does them will be similar to a wise man who built his house on the rock. And the rain came down and the rivers came and the strong winds blew and fell upon that house and it did not fall for it had been built on the rock. And all who hear these words of mine and is not practicing them, will be similar to a foolish man who built his house on sand. And the rain came down and the rivers came and the winds blew and beat against that house and it fell; and great was its fall. And it happened that when Jesus finished these words the crowds were amazed at his teaching. For he was teaching them as one having authority and not as their scribes.

Key verse: *"And the rain came down and the rivers came and the strong winds blew and fell upon that house and it did not fall for it had been built on the rock."* (Matt 7:25)

Jesus closes his sermon with an illustration of two houses. The differences between the houses are the builders and the foundations that they chose. The person that listens to Jesus' teaching and does them is compared to a wise man who builds his house on a solid rock, giving it a strong foundation. The person that hears Jesus' saying and does not do them is like a foolish (*mōros*)[21] man that built his house on sand, giving it a weak foundation. The rains and winds fell upon both houses; the one built on the rock stood whereas the one built on sand collapsed.

There is a different word choice in verse 27 than what was used in verse 25. In verse 27, the word refers to a more "violent strike" as opposed to the previous word for "falling upon" in verse 25. The words sound similar in Greek: *prospipto* (fell upon),

---

[21] The Greek word used here is the root for the English word moron.

and *proskopto* (beat against). The word choices show the different ways the two houses *experienced* the same storm (fell upon verses beat against). The strong house felt the storm, but did not experience any structural damage. The other house took a beating and was destroyed. The difference between the houses were their foundations.

The stormy weather can represents the common trials of earthly life. We will all experience difficult moments in our lives. The difference is whether we choose to abide by the words of Christ or not. Both men in the illustration heard the words of Jesus but only one practiced them. The one that choose not to obey still built a house, but chose the wrong foundation. Perhaps there were some things that house would have been able to endure. But the violent storm that beat against the house was able to tear it down. There are some heartaches and pain that we can only endure through Christ. In Him we know that we have eternal life. Through Him we understand that this world is not all there is. Because He lives, we know that we will also live (*John 14:19*). The famous hymn by Edward Mote illustrates this external hope that we have:

My hope is built on nothing less
Than Jesus' blood and righteousness;
I dare not trust the sweetest frame,
But wholly trust in Jesus' Name.

Refrain:

On Christ the solid Rock I stand;
All other ground is sinking sand,
All other ground is sinking sand.

When darkness seems to hide His face,
I rest on His unchanging grace;
In every high and stormy gale,
My anchor holds within the veil.

His oath, His covenant, His blood,
Support me in the whelming flood;
When all around my soul gives way,
He then is all my Hope and Stay.

When He shall come with trumpet sound,
Oh may I then in Him be found;
Dressed in His righteousness alone,
Faultless to stand before the throne.

Prayer: *"In and through the storms of life, Lord help me to hold on to you."*

Reflection: *"Consider the analogy of the two houses. Why would a house need a strong foundation if there were never a storm? Should we pray for God to remove the storms from our lives? Or should we trust God for strength in the midst of the storm?*

CLOSING REMARKS

You could read The Sermon on the Mount in one sitting. If you took your time, you could probably read all one-hundred and eleven verses in under twenty-minutes. In reality, it took Jesus much longer to preach the sermon than it does for us to read through it. We can only imagine Jesus' pace of speaking, the tone and pitch of his voice, and points of emphasis. We can visualize his eye contact and body language as he expounded certain points. With so much of Jesus' life and ministry to cover, Matthew can only grant us a compact version of the sermon. Still, there is so much to reflect on.

It is more beneficial to read through the sermon slowly. As we have seen, Jesus covers a multitude of topics. He challenges his followers to have high moral character: we are to break away from sin, guard our tongues, honor our marriage covenant, love our enemies, and examine our motives. Jesus also outlines the true practice of religion: we are to let our light shine with good works, store up treasures in heaven, endure hardships, let our devotion be for God's eyes only, and not worship God while holding grudges against others.

Jesus concludes the sermon with a word of encouragement for his followers. When we obey Jesus, we build a strong foundation for our lives. (Notice it is not enough to listen to his words, but we must actually do them). Obeying the words of Christ does not prevent difficulties in life. However, with Jesus as our foundation, we make certain that we are still standing after the storm has passed. Amen.

APPENDIX A:
MATTHEW 19:3 - 12

And Pharisees came to [Jesus] and tested him by asking, "Is it lawful for a man to divorce his wife for any reason[22]?" But [Jesus] answered and said, "Have you not read that the one who created them made them male and female, and said, Therefore, a man will leave his father and mother and is glued to his wife, and the two will become one flesh? Thus, they are no longer two but one flesh. Therefore, what God has joined together a man must not separate."

[Then] they answered [Jesus], "But why did Moses command to give her a certificate of divorce and release her?" [Jesus] said to them, "Because of your hard hearts, Moses allowed you to divorce your wives. But in the

---

[22] The adjective translated "any" can also be translated as "all" or "every". The question centered upon the range of offences for which a man could legally divorce his wife. The question can be understood as: "Can a man divorce his wife for any reason (big or small)?"

beginning, it was not this way. But I say to you that whoever divorces his wife, unless it is over sexually immorality, and marries another commits adultery."

The disciples said to [Jesus], "If this is the case of a man with his wife, it is better not to marry!"[23] But [Jesus] replied to them, "Not everyone can receive this word, but only those to whom it has been given. For there are some who were eunuchs from their mother's womb, and some who were made eunuchs by men, and some who became eunuchs themselves for the kingdom of heaven. The one able to receive this, should receive it."[24]

---

[23] This is a remarkable statement by the disciples and highlights the mindset of the culture. In their minds, if a man could not dismiss his wife whenever he saw fit, it was better to not get married at all! Later teachings by Paul indicate that the church began to teach and understand that marriage was a binding covenant not to be broken over trivial matters (see 1 Cor. 7:12 - 16; and 7:39).

[24] Jesus understands that most of us desire and need the companionship and physical intimacy that comes with marriage. There are a few people, however, who have been specially gifted by God. They can live a fulfilled single life and focus all of their attention on serving God.

CPSIA information can be obtained
at www.ICGtesting.com
Printed in the USA
BVHW031502011020
590077BV00006B/309

9 781663 200730